R. VAUGHAN WILLIAMS

SERENADE IN A MINOR

(1898)

EDITED BY

JULIAN RUSHTON

STUDY SCORE

MUSIC DEPARTMENT

OXFORD

UNIVERSITY PRESS

CONTENTS

PREFACE

In the months following his marriage to Adeline Fisher on 9 October 1897, Ralph Vaughan Williams undertook two substantial compositional projects: his degree exercise for the Cambridge University doctorate (a partial Mass setting with orchestral accompaniment) and his first completed orchestral work, the *Serenade for Small Orchestra in A minor*. A number of letters, not all of them precisely dated, refer to progress on this work. Two were sent from 19 Second Avenue, Brighton, where the Vaughan Williams couple lived for part of 1898, following a visit to Germany, and while seeking a home in London. Adeline Vaughan Williams wrote to René Gatty: 'Ralph has just signed the lease & we are furnishing our house as soon as possible—he is writing a new Serenade for orchestra, wh. is turning out very Dvorak-y'. The other is to Gustav Holst; Vaughan Williams wrote that he had been 'scoring my Mass all day ... I am approaching the end of the Credo', and continued:

> Did I ever tell you of my final talk with Stanford in which we agreed that if I *added* a short movement in E major in the middle & altered the Coda the thing might stand—I had already got an extra movement in E major which I had cut out! [1]

This presumably refers to the third of the *Serenade*'s five movements, which is indeed short and in E major.[2] What must be a slightly later letter was sent to Holst from 5 Cowley Street, Westminster, where the couple were living in the summer of 1898: 'I have written a new coda and a new movement for my Serenade and most of my degree exercise'.[3]

This new movement may be the fourth ('Romance'), which is in some ways the most strikingly original in conception.[4] The autograph score, however, does not confirm the order of composition, being a fair copy clearly laid out as a work in five movements.

The autograph is signed by Vaughan Williams with the address 10 Barton Street, Westminster, where Kennedy states that he lived 'from early 1899 to November 1905'. The address and revisions to the title-page were no doubt added some time before the first performance, together with the note at the end of the score: 'Written 1897–8'. Various musical revisions were presumably made after hearing the work at rehearsal at the Royal College of Music.

Adeline Vaughan Williams wrote to their cousin that 'Stanford after practising his Serenade diligently at 3 rehearsals threw it up for no apparent reason, so now it is trying its luck at the Crystal Palace—we expect to see it return with "not wanted" on it every day.'[5] This prediction was evidently accurate. The first performance took place in the Bournemouth Winter Gardens on 4 April 1901.[6] It was given by the Bournemouth Municipal Orchestra, conducted by Dan Godfrey, one of his many premieres of works by British composers. The Bournemouth Municipal Orchestra was founded in 1893 with 24 regular players, and numbers steadily increased, with extra players engaged as necessary.[7] The programme for the 1902 concert that included Vaughan Williams's *Bucolic Suite* lists 40 players, of whom 21 were strings.[8] In the *Serenade* Vaughan Williams requires eight woodwind, four brass, and timpani.[9] Hadley Watkins mentions 45 players for October 1901 with extras as required.[10] This fits the 'small orchestra' of the title, although the Bournemouth players undertook symphonic repertory usually given with larger forces. It is possible the work was tried over on a Thursday afternoon rather than included in the more prestigious series of evening concerts. A further performance took place in London (Aeolian Hall) on 3 March 1908, conducted by Rosabel Watson.

Vaughan Williams writes throughout for horns in F and trumpets in A without key-signature. In this edition the trumpets are written in C. Some variation may have been made to Vaughan Williams's instrumentation; in the 'Romance', at bar 141, the important second trumpet entry is cued (no doubt by the conductor) with the word 'cornet'.

The first movement has no title; it is called 'Prelude' by Michael Kennedy. In the autograph score the 'Trio' of the third movement is crossed out and 'Omit the Trio' is written above in pencil. Since the passage is neither long nor difficult the cut may have been made because someone—perhaps Vaughan Williams himself—thought it less good than the rest. It is included in this edition, and if performed is followed by the first part of the movement *da capo*. This edition separates the first- and second-time bars; in the source, both versions are written in a single bar, the whole-bar rests marked '1st time' and the rests plus chord marked '2nd time'. No third version is suggested to follow the *da capo*. Possibly Vaughan Williams only intended the additional chord for the end of the movement (whether or not the Trio is included); and it is also possible that he did not intend a fermata before taking the repeat. Performers may, therefore, select from the possible interpretations of the notation.

Julian Rushton

iv

END NOTES

[1] The Mass consists only of Credo, Offertorium, Sanctus and Benedictus. The Credo therefore amounts to something like half the work (my thanks to Alan Tongue for this information).

[2] The letter has been dated 1897: Ursula Vaughan Williams and Imogen Holst (eds.), *Heirs and Rebels* (London: Oxford University Press, 1959), letter 1, p. 1. But it evidently followed the visit to Germany in 1898; Hugh Cobbe (ed.), *Letters of Ralph Vaughan Williams 1895–1958* (Oxford: Oxford University Press, 2008), pp. 34–5. My thanks to Hugh Cobbe for the text of this and other letters.

[3] Cited in Michael Kennedy, *The Works of Ralph Vaughan Williams* (London: Oxford University Press, 1964), p. 400; Kennedy, *A Catalogue of the Works of Ralph Vaughan Williams* (Oxford: Oxford University Press, 1996), p. 7. All Kennedy references are to these pages.

[4] Kennedy describes the 'new movement' as an 'alternative third movement' but only after the 'Trio' of the third movement is cancelled in the score.

[5] Letter to Ralph [Randolph] Wedgewood, dated 15 December, without a year (presumably 1899). My thanks to Hugh Cobbe for supplying the full text; this letter is quoted in Kennedy's *Catalogue* but not in *The Works of Ralph Vaughan Williams*.

[6] In a letter to Edwin Evans probably of 1903, Vaughan Williams includes the Serenade among his 'most important works'.

[7] The figure of 24 players is from Geoffrey Miller, *The Bournemouth Symphony Orchestra* (Sherborne: Dorset Publishing Company, 1970), p. 27. In his memoirs the conductor gives the 1893 figure as 33 (Sir Dan Godfrey, *Memories and Music. Thirty-five Years of Conducting* (London: Hutchinson, 1924), p. 284.

[8] I am grateful for the help of Carolyn Butterworth (Bournemouth Libraries) and Andrew Burn (Bournemouth Symphony Orchestra). No corresponding programme has surfaced for the *Serenade* performance.

[9] Kennedy's list assumes 27 strings (probably divided 8/8/4/4/3). This is possible if there were 45 players available (trombones and tuba are not employed in the *Serenade*). No string numbers are prescribed in the autograph score.

[10] Hadley Watkins, *The Bournemouth Municipal Orchestra: A Souvenir Record of Growth and Development with Chronologia of Chief Events* (Bournemouth, 1914), p. 34. Watkins does not mention Vaughan Williams's *Serenade* or *Bucolic Suite* among important events, and fails to include Vaughan Williams in the list of 'visits of British Composers'.

SOURCE

MS holograph full score, Yale University Library Osborn Music MS 505 (Gift of Thomas M. Osborn). Music pp. 1–122, with blank versos between movements, through paginated by the composer. The pagination works out as follows: I. Andante sostenuto, 1–17 (18 blank); II. Scherzo (Allegro), 19–46; III. Intermezzo and Trio (Allegretto), 47–59 (60 blank); IV. Romance (Andantino), 61–89 (90 blank); V. Finale (Allegro), 91–122.

The title page contains several alterations. At the top of the page, 'R. Vaughan Williams Serenade' is crossed out. The definitive title is placed in the centre of the page:

Serenade / for small [inserted] orchestra / in A minor / by / Ralph Vaughan Williams / [At the foot, RH], 10 Barton St / Westminster / London / SW

Above this, presumably added at the time of performance: '25 minutes' (25 replacing 26). Below the title, stuck-on paper has been torn away; just visible is the date, '13.4.1901' when perhaps the composer tidied the score after the first performance on 4 April 1901.[1] The first page of music (p. 1) is titled 'Serenade for Orchestra / in A minor / R. Vaughan Williams'.

The MS is of 24-stave paper, used as follows throughout: 1–7 blank, 8 Flauti; 9 Oboi; 10 Clarinetti; 11 Fagotti; 12 blank; 13 Corni; 14 Trombe; 15 Tympani [with the pitches for the first movement given in a preparatory stave]; 16 blank; 17 Violini I^{mi}; 18 Violini II^{mi}; 19 Viole; 20 Violoncelli; 21 Contrabassi; 22–4 blank.

The text is essentially a fair copy, with a few revisions (see Textual Notes). It was evidently used by the conductor (Dan Godfrey), who was probably responsible for numerous markings in crayon (mainly blue). These include crossing out the Trio to the intermezzo. The majority are scaled down dynamics, cues, and memoranda (at the end of the first movement, 'Wait for Trumpets').

---

[1] I am grateful to J. P. E. Harper-Scott who provided these data.

TEXTUAL NOTES

Abbreviations: S = the source, Yale University Library Osborn Music MS 505.

Instrument names are as in the score: Fl., Ob., Cl., Bsn., Hrn., Tpt., Timp., Vln. I, II, Vla., Vlc., Cb.; where instruments share a staff, the comment applies to both unless otherwise stated.

References are to bars. Where necessary pitches are referred to as follows:

C2 C3 B♯3 C♭4 A4 C5 C6

Note values: c = crotchet, c. = dotted crotchet, cr = crotchet rest; q = quaver, qr = quaver rest; sq = semiquaver.

Some minor discrepancies in the source are evidently oversights or errors. In this edition, redundant accidentals are omitted, as are some redundant dynamics; these and obviously incorrect note-values or rests are adjusted without comment. Some defective dynamics and articulation have been provided, without typographical distinction, by reference to other parts. Vaughan Williams changes unnecessarily often from bass to tenor clef (Bsn., Vlc.); some of these changes have been eliminated. Minor inconsistencies in such matters as beaming are reconciled, but essentially Vaughan Williams's beaming practices are retained.

Where no direct parallels can be made, editorial dynamics and instrumental specifications are in square brackets: [*p*], [1]. Editorial slurs and *cresc./dim.* hairpins are dotted. Where a reading has been inferred (as for instance in the case of missing dots or rests) or seems to need adjustment, the original reading is indicated below.

Rehearsal letters are those that appear in the source. An isolated fingering (Romance, bar 30, first violins, '3' at the marking 'sul G') has been omitted.

I. Prelude

11	Vlc.: S has a single slur; adjusted to bar 4 slurs
12	Timp.: S rolls over whole bar (including the rest)
27	Vla.: S has cresc. under 2nd beat, not 3rd

35	Tpt.: S slur covers all three notes
38	Ob. 2 assumed; S has down tails only
40	In S, several parts have a second *cresc.*, omitted as unnecessary
48	Bsn., Hrn., strings: S repeats *pp*
49–50	Vln. II: in S, these notes are lightly crossed out
51	Vla., Vlc.: unis. markings as in S
56, 58	Strings: double slurs as in S
58	Cb.: S has D3
60–1	Strings: S slur begins only at 61 (cf. the opening and 54–5).
62	Ob., Cl., Bsn., Hrn., Tpt.: slurs are editorial
67	Cb.: dynamics as in S
68	Timp.: continuation of roll editorial, implied by tie

II. Scherzo

1	Tpt.: S: one stem; unis. assumed
17	Ob.: S lacks rest
17	Woodwind: S lacks slurs (cf. bar 124)
18	Ob. 1: S second note G4
18	Hrn. 1: S lacks ♯
18	Vla.: S, 4th note chord C4/E4; C4 omitted
20	Cl.: S notes 2–4 one stem; a 2 assumed as bar 131
21	Vln. II: S first chord bottom note E3 not G3; lacks D4
23	Fl. 1: D6 is clear in S; but cf. 134
23	Bsn.: S second note C3
23–4	Woodwind: S lacks articulation (cf. 134–5)
25	Fl. 2: S 4th note E5
25	Bsn. 2: S has 1st note C3 not E3
25	Vla.: S C3 not E3 in chord (cf. bar 136)
25	Vlc., Cb.: S last note stacc.
28–9	Bsn., Hrn.: S lacks 'a 2'
48	Ob.: S stacc.
48	Vln. II: S chord C4/G4
65	Vla.: S lacks qr; first note altered from c
80	Vln. II: S slurs only to F
91	Vln. II: S first three E4s written D4
109–11	Vla.: S notation suggests repeated notes (chords) rather than tremolo
131	Tpt. 2: S 2nd beat q E4 (cf. horns and bar 20)
131	Vlc.: S 'col basso' so E3 not E2 (cf. bar 20)
132	Cl.1: S second note D5 (cf. bar 21)
132	Vln. I: S lacks lower notes of second chord
132	Vln. II: S lacks G3 (cf. bar 21)

133	Tpt. 2: S has q G4 on 2nd beat (cf. horns and bar 22)	92	S accents only in Fl., Ob. 1
134	Vla.: S lacks lower notes of chord	95	S accents only Fl., Bsn. 2, Hrn., Tpt., Vcl., Cb.
135	Cl. 2: S q qr qr for c qr (cf. bar 24)	102	Vln. II, Vla.: S repeats *p*
136	Bsn. 2: S has 1st note C3 not E3	103	Woodwind: in S a small slur connects grace-notes to the triplet (also 105, 109)
136	Hrn. 2: 2nd note q A3		
136	Vlc., Cb.: S lacks qr	105	Ob., Bsn.: S lacks accent (also 107, Bsn.)
137	Ob. 2: S has 1st note E4	105–6	Vln. II, Vla.: S begins slur from last note of 105, not completed in 106 after page-turn; probably a copying error
137	Cl.: 1st note, S has C5 not D5 (cf. bar 26)		
138	Bsn.: 2nd time, S has only upper E (double stem)		
150	Vlc.: S ♯ on 3rd note, not the first	109–10	Vln. II: S div. only in 110
189	Hrn.: S single stem; a 2 assumed	125	Ob. 1: in S, G4 revised to A4; no rest, no B4
191	Vlc., Cb.: S 4th note c, followed by qr	130	Vlc.: S, slur over q and triplet
		133–4	Vln. I: S, slurs do not cover grace-notes

III. Intermezzo and Trio

		135	Vln. I: sqr: qr assumed
12	Woodwind: S lacks slurs on first two notes (also 29, Fl.)		
23	Vln. II: S last note lacks natural		**V. Finale**
37	S does not separate first- and second-time bars; see Preface	9	Vln. II, Vla., Vlc., S *f* repeated on second note and first Cb. qr
52	S lacks articulation in all wind instruments	10	Ob. 2: S second note A4
		12	Hrn. 1: S lacks ♯

IV. Romance

		16	Cl., Bsn., Hrn.: S lacks accent
38	Ob.: S lacks hairpins	33	Fl., Cl., Tpt.: S *cresc.*, rather than hairpin *cresc.*
43	Vln. 1: S slurs first three sqs only	88	Vlc.: S slur not extended into 89; adjusted to Cb.
49	Ob. and similar passages, beaming as in S	173–6	Vla.: in S, added later (rests deleted); *dim.* hairpin starts earlier; aligned with Cl.
53–79	Vla.: S on one staff		
74	Vla. I: S lacks tie	187	Bsn. 1: S first note C♯3
89	Hrn. 1: S has F not G, although tied over the page-turn	200–1	Cb.: in S, colla Vcl.; lower pitches assumed
		204	Fl. 2, Hrn. 2: D5 (Hrn. notated A4)

SERENADE

ORCHESTRATION

2 Flutes

2 Oboes

2 Clarinets

2 Bassoons

2 Horns

2 Trumpets

Timpani

Strings

Duration: *c*.25 minutes

Serenade (1898) for Small Orchestra

I Prelude

RALPH VAUGHAN WILLIAMS

5

II Scherzo

43

III Intermezzo and Trio

56

Fine

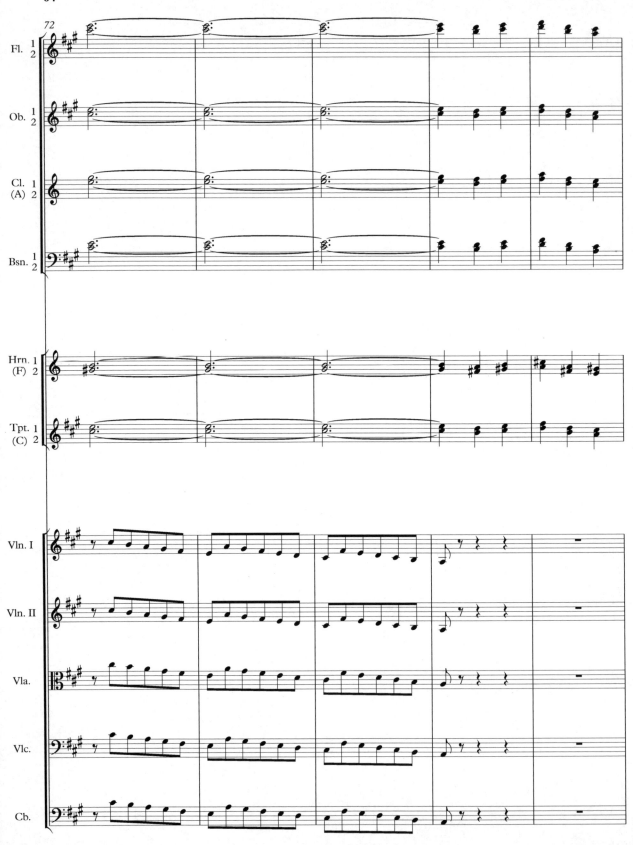

Intermezzo da capo sin al Fine

Intermezzo da capo sin al Fine

IV Romance

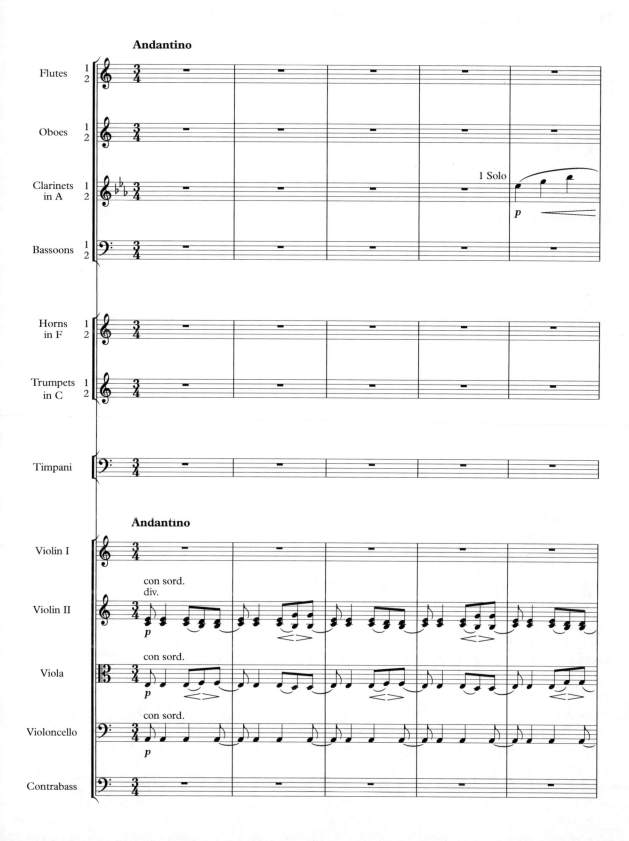

121
Fl. 1 2
Ob. 1 2
Cl. 1 2 (A)
Bsn. 1 2
Hrn. 1 2 (F)
Tpt. 1 2 (C)
Timp.
Vln. I
Vln. II
Vla.
Vlc.
Cb.
(1)
3
f
pp
tr
2
[div.]

131

V Finale

104

un poco meno mosso